table of contents

burgundy beef po' boys
with dipping sauce   4

suzie's sloppy joes   6

pulled pork sliders
with cola barbecue sauce   8

hot and juicy reuben
sandwiches   10

chicken and brie sandwiches   12

shredded apricot pork
sandwiches   14

open-face provençal
vegetable sandwich   16

italian beef   18

tavern burger   18

pork tenderloin sliders   20

mini swiss steak
sandwiches   22

chipotle turkey sloppy joe
sliders   24

root beer bbq pulled pork   26

southwestern salmon
po' boys   28

best beef brisket
sandwich ever   30

easy homemade barbecue
sandwiches   32

barbecued beef sandwiches   34

shredded pork roast   36

cheeseburger sloppy joes   38

hot beef sandwiches   40

sloppy joe sliders   40

cuban pork sandwiches   42

super meatball sliders   44

big al's hot and sweet
sausage sandwiches   46

bbq pulled chicken
sandwiches   46

barbecue beef sliders   48

italian meatball hoagies   50

hot beef sandwiches au jus   52

meatless sloppy joes   54

green chile pulled pork
sandwiches   56

hoisin barbecue chicken
sliders   58

sloppy sloppy joes   60

barbecued pulled pork
sandwiches   62

burgundy beef po' boys with dipping sauce

Makes 6 to 8 servings

- 2 cups chopped onions
- 1 boneless beef chuck shoulder or bottom round roast (about 3 pounds), trimmed*
- ¼ cup dry red wine
- 3 tablespoons balsamic vinegar
- 1 tablespoon beef bouillon granules
- 1 tablespoon Worcestershire sauce
- ¾ teaspoon dried thyme
- ½ teaspoon garlic powder
- Italian rolls, warmed and split

*Unless you have a 5-, 6- or 7-quart **CROCK-POT®** slow cooker, cut any roast larger than 2½ pounds in half so it cooks completely.*

1. Place onions in bottom of **CROCK-POT®** slow cooker. Top with beef, wine, vinegar, bouillon granules, Worcestershire sauce, thyme and garlic powder. Cover; cook on HIGH 8 to 10 hours.

2. Turn off heat. Remove beef to large cutting board; shred with two forks. Let cooking liquid stand 5 minutes. Skim off fat and discard. Spoon beef onto rolls. Serve with cooking liquid as dipping sauce.

suzie's sloppy joes

Makes 8 servings

- 3 pounds ground beef
- 1 cup chopped onion
- 3 cloves garlic, minced
- 1¼ cups ketchup
- 1 cup chopped red bell pepper
- ¼ cup plus 1 tablespoon Worcestershire sauce
- ¼ cup packed dark brown sugar
- 3 tablespoons prepared mustard
- 3 tablespoons vinegar
- 2 teaspoons chili powder
- 8 hamburger buns, toasted

1. Brown beef, onion and garlic in large nonstick skillet over medium-high heat 6 to 8 minutes, stirring to break up meat. Remove beef mixture to **CROCK-POT**® slow cooker using slotted spoon.

2. Add ketchup, bell pepper, Worcestershire sauce, brown sugar, mustard, vinegar and chili powder to **CROCK-POT**® slow cooker; stir to blend. Cover; cook on LOW 6 to 8 hours. Serve on buns.

pulled pork sliders with cola barbecue sauce

Makes 16 sliders

1 teaspoon vegetable oil

3 pounds boneless pork shoulder roast, cut evenly into 4 pieces

1 cup cola

¼ cup tomato paste

2 tablespoons packed brown sugar

2 teaspoons Worcestershire sauce

2 teaspoons spicy brown mustard

Hot pepper sauce

Salt

16 dinner rolls or potato rolls

Sliced pickles (optional)

1. Heat oil in large skillet over medium-high heat. Add pork; cook 5 to 7 minutes or until browned on all sides. Remove to **CROCK-POT®** slow cooker. Pour cola over pork. Cover; cook on LOW 7½ to 8 hours or on HIGH 3½ to 4 hours.

2. Turn off heat. Remove pork to large cutting board; shred with two forks. Let cooking liquid stand 5 minutes. Skim off fat and discard. Whisk tomato paste, brown sugar, Worcestershire sauce and mustard into **CROCK-POT®** slow cooker. Cover; cook on HIGH 15 minutes or until thickened.

3. Stir shredded pork into **CROCK-POT®** slow cooker. Season with hot pepper sauce and salt. Serve on rolls. Top with pickles, if desired.

hot and juicy reuben sandwiches

Makes 4 servings

- 1 corned beef, trimmed (about 1½ pounds)
- 2 cups sauerkraut, drained
- ½ cup beef broth
- 1 small onion, sliced
- 1 clove garlic, minced
- ¼ teaspoon caraway seeds
- 4 to 6 black peppercorns
- 8 slices pumpernickel or rye bread
- 4 slices Swiss cheese
  Prepared mustard

1. Place corned beef in **CROCK-POT**® slow cooker. Add sauerkraut, broth, onion, garlic, caraway seeds and peppercorns. Cover; cook on LOW 7 to 9 hours.

2. Remove beef to large cutting board. Cut beef across grain into 16 slices. Divide evenly among 4 slices of bread. Top each slice with ½ cup drained sauerkraut mixture and 1 slice cheese. Spread mustard on remaining 4 bread slices; place on sandwiches.

chicken and brie sandwiches

Makes 6 servings

- 1 red bell pepper, chopped
- 1 to 2 carrots, sliced
- ½ cup sliced celery
- 1 onion, chopped
- 1 clove garlic, minced
- ¼ teaspoon dried oregano
- ¼ teaspoon red pepper flakes
- ¼ cup all-purpose flour
- 1 teaspoon salt
- ½ teaspoon black pepper
- 6 boneless, skinless chicken thighs or breasts
- 1 tablespoon vegetable oil
- 1 can (about 14 ounces) chicken broth
- 6 sub rolls, split and toasted or 2 thin baguettes (about 12 ounces *each*), split and toasted
- 1 large wedge brie cheese, cut into 12 pieces

1. Place bell pepper, carrots, celery, onion, garlic, oregano and red pepper flakes in **CROCK-POT**® slow cooker.

2. Combine flour, salt and black pepper in large resealable food storage bag. Add chicken, 2 pieces at a time; shake to coat with flour mixture. Heat oil in large skillet over medium-high heat. Add chicken; cook 6 to 8 minutes or until browned on both sides.

3. Place chicken over vegetables in **CROCK-POT**® slow cooker; add broth. Cover; cook on LOW 5 to 6 hours.

4. Remove chicken from **CROCK-POT**® slow cooker, thinly slice and arrange on sub rolls. Spoon 1 to 2 tablespoons broth mixture over chicken and top with cheese.

shredded apricot pork sandwiches

Makes 10 to 12 sandwiches

- 1 boneless pork top loin roast (4 pounds)*
- 2 onions, thinly sliced
- 1 cup apricot preserves
- ½ cup packed dark brown sugar
- ½ cup barbecue sauce
- ¼ cup cider vinegar
- 2 tablespoons Worcestershire sauce
- ½ teaspoon red pepper flakes
- ¼ cup water
- 2 tablespoons cornstarch
- 1 tablespoon grated fresh ginger
- 1 teaspoon salt
- 1 teaspoon black pepper
- 10 to 12 sesame or onion rolls, toasted

*Unless you have a 5-, 6- or 7-quart **CROCK-POT**® slow cooker, cut any roast larger than 2½ pounds in half so it cooks completely.*

1. Combine pork, onions, preserves, brown sugar, barbecue sauce, vinegar, Worcestershire sauce and red pepper flakes in **CROCK-POT**® slow cooker. Cover; cook on LOW 8 to 9 hours.

2. Turn off heat. Remove pork to large cutting board; shred with two forks. Let cooking liquid stand 5 minutes. Skim off fat and discard.

3. Turn **CROCK-POT**® slow cooker to HIGH. Stir water into cornstarch in small bowl until smooth. Stir in ginger, salt and black pepper. Whisk cornstarch mixture into sauce. Cook, uncovered, on HIGH 15 to 30 minutes or until sauce is thickened. Return pork to **CROCK-POT**® slow cooker; stir to blend. Serve on rolls.

open-face provençal vegetable sandwich

Makes 6 servings

 2 cups sliced shiitake mushroom caps
 1 large zucchini, halved lengthwise and sliced ¼ inch thick
 1 large red bell pepper, quartered lengthwise and thinly sliced
 1 small onion, sliced lengthwise ¼ inch thick
 1 small jalapeño pepper, seeded and minced*
 ¼ cup vegetable broth
 ¼ cup pitted kalamata olives
 2 tablespoons capers
 1 clove garlic, minced
1½ tablespoons olive oil, divided
 ½ teaspoon dried oregano
    Salt and black pepper
 4 teaspoons white wine vinegar
    Crusty bread, cut into thick slices

Jalapeño peppers can sting and irritate the skin, so wear rubber gloves when handling peppers and do not touch your eyes.

1. Combine mushrooms, zucchini, bell pepper, onion, jalapeño pepper, broth, olives, capers, garlic, 1 tablespoon oil, oregano, salt and black pepper in **CROCK-POT®** slow cooker; stir to blend. Cover; cook on LOW 5 to 6 hours.

2. Turn off heat. Stir in vinegar and remaining ½ tablespoon oil. Let stand, uncovered, 15 to 30 minutes or until vegetables absorb some liquid. (Vegetable mixture should be lukewarm.) Season with additional salt and black pepper, if desired. Spoon vegetables onto bread.

italian beef

Makes 8 servings

  1 boneless beef rump roast (3 to 5 pounds)*
  1 can (about 14 ounces) beef broth
  2 cups mild giardiniera
  8 crusty Italian bread rolls, split

Unless you have a 5-, 6- or 7-quart **CROCK-POT® slow cooker, cut any roast larger than 2½ pounds in half so it cooks completely.*

1. Place beef in **CROCK-POT**® slow cooker; add broth and giardiniera. Cover; cook on LOW 10 hours.

2. Remove beef to large cutting board; shred with two forks. Return beef to cooking liquid; stir to blend. To serve, spoon beef and sauce onto rolls.

tavern burger

Makes 8 servings

  2 pounds ground beef
  ½ cup ketchup
  ¼ cup packed brown sugar
  ¼ cup yellow mustard
  8 hamburger buns

1. Brown beef in large skillet over medium-high heat 6 to 8 minutes, stirring to break up meat. Remove beef mixture to **CROCK-POT**® slow cooker using slotted spoon.

2. Add ketchup, brown sugar and mustard to **CROCK-POT**® slow cooker; stir to blend. Cover; cook on LOW 4 to 6 hours. Serve on buns.

Tip: This is also known to some people as "BBQs" or "loose-meat sandwiches." For added flavor, add a can of pork and beans when adding the other ingredients.

italian beef

pork tenderloin sliders

Makes 12 sandwiches

- ½ cup mayonnaise
- 1 canned chipotle pepper in adobo sauce, minced
- 2 teaspoons lime juice
- 2 teaspoons chili powder
- ¾ teaspoon ground cumin
- ½ teaspoon salt
- ½ teaspoon black pepper
- 2 tablespoons olive oil, divided
- 2 pork tenderloins (about 1 pound *each*)
- 2 cups chicken broth
- 12 green onions, ends trimmed
- 12 dinner rolls, sliced in half horizontally
- 12 slices Monterey Jack cheese

1. Coat inside of **CROCK-POT**® slow cooker with nonstick cooking spray. Combine mayonnaise, chipotle pepper and lime juice is small bowl; stir to blend. Cover and refrigerate.

2. Combine chili powder, cumin, salt and black pepper in small bowl. Rub 1 tablespoon oil evenly over pork. Sprinkle cumin mixture evenly over tenderloins, turning to coat. Heat large skillet over medium heat. Add tenderloins; cook 7 to 10 minutes or until browned on all sides. Remove to **CROCK-POT**® slow cooker. Add broth and green onions. Cover; cook on LOW 6 to 8 hours.

3. Remove pork and green onions to large cutting board. Coarsely chop green onions. Thinly slice pork. Evenly spread chipotle mayonnaise on bottom halves of rolls. Top with green onions, tenderloin slices, cheese and roll tops.

mini swiss steak sandwiches

Makes 16 to 18 servings

  2 tablespoons all-purpose flour
 ¼ teaspoon salt
 ¼ teaspoon black pepper
 1¾ pounds boneless beef chuck steak, about 1 inch thick
  2 tablespoons vegetable oil
  1 medium onion, sliced
  1 green bell pepper, sliced
  1 clove garlic, sliced
  1 cup stewed tomatoes
 ¾ cup beef broth
  2 teaspoons Worcestershire sauce
  1 whole bay leaf
  2 tablespoons cornstarch
  2 packages (12 ounces *each*) sweet Hawaiian-style dinner rolls

1. Coat inside of **CROCK-POT®** slow cooker with nonstick cooking spray. Combine flour, salt and black pepper in large resealable food storage bag. Add steak. Seal bag; shake to coat. Heat oil in large skillet over high heat. Add steak; cook 5 to 7 minutes or until browned on both sides. Remove to **CROCK-POT®** slow cooker.

2. Add onion and bell pepper to skillet; cook and stir over medium-high heat 3 minutes or until softened. Add garlic; cook and stir 30 seconds. Pour mixture over steak. Add tomatoes, broth, Worcestershire sauce and bay leaf to **CROCK-POT®** slow cooker. Cover; cook on HIGH 3½ hours.

3. Turn off heat. Remove steak to large cutting board; shred with two forks. Remove and discard bay leaf. Let cooking liquid stand 5 minutes. Skim off fat and discard. Stir 2 tablespoons cooking liquid into cornstarch in small bowl until smooth; whisk into cooking liquid in **CROCK-POT®** slow cooker. Cover; cook on HIGH 10 minutes or until thickened.

4. Return steak to **CROCK-POT®** slow cooker; stir to blend. Serve steak mixture on rolls.

Tip: Browning meat before cooking it in the **CROCK-POT®** slow cooker is not necessary, but helps to enhance the flavor and appearance of the finished dish.

chipotle turkey sloppy joe sliders

Makes 12 sliders

- 1 pound turkey Italian sausage, casings removed
- 1 package (14 ounces) frozen green and red bell pepper strips with onions
- 1 can (6 ounces) tomato paste
- 1 tablespoon quick-cooking tapioca
- 1 tablespoon minced canned chipotle peppers in adobo sauce, plus 1 tablespoon sauce
- 2 teaspoons ground cumin
- ½ teaspoon dried thyme
- 12 corn muffins or small dinner rolls, split and toasted

1. Brown sausage in large skillet over medium-high heat 6 to 8 minutes, stirring to break up meat. Remove to **CROCK-POT**® slow cooker using slotted spoon.

2. Stir in pepper strips with onions, tomato paste, tapioca, chipotle peppers with sauce, cumin and thyme. Cover; cook on LOW 8 to 10 hours. Serve on corn muffins.

root beer bbq pulled pork

Makes 8 servings

1 can (12 ounces) root beer
1 bottle (18 ounces) sweet barbecue sauce, divided
1 package (1 ounce) dry onion soup mix
1 (6- to 8-pound) boneless pork shoulder roast*
    Salt and black pepper
    Hamburger buns

Unless you have a 5-, 6- or 7-quart **CROCK-POT® slow cooker, cut any roast larger than 2½ pounds in half so it cooks completely.*

1. Coat inside of **CROCK-POT**® slow cooker with nonstick cooking spray. Combine root beer and ½ bottle barbecue sauce in medium bowl. Rub dry soup mix on pork roast. Place barbecue mixture and roast in **CROCK-POT**® slow cooker. Cover; cook on LOW 8 to 10 hours.

2. Remove pork to large cutting board; shred with two forks. Reserve 1 cup barbecue mixture in **CROCK-POT**® slow cooker; discard remaining mixture. Turn **CROCK-POT**® slow cooker to HIGH. Stir shredded pork, remaining ½ bottle barbecue sauce, salt and pepper into **CROCK-POT**® slow cooker. Cover; cook on HIGH 20 minutes or until heated through. Serve on buns.

southwestern salmon po' boys

Makes 4 servings

1 red bell pepper, sliced
1 green bell pepper, sliced
1 onion, sliced
½ teaspoon Southwest chipotle seasoning
¼ teaspoon salt
¼ teaspoon black pepper
4 salmon fillets (about 6 ounces *each*), rinsed and patted dry
½ cup Italian dressing
¼ cup water
4 large French sandwich rolls, split and toasted
Chipotle mayonnaise*
Fresh cilantro (optional)

If unavailable, combine ¼ cup mayonnaise with ½ teaspoon adobo sauce or substitute regular mayonnaise.

1. Coat inside of **CROCK-POT**® slow cooker with nonstick cooking spray. Arrange half of sliced bell peppers and onion in bottom.

2. Combine seasoning, salt and black pepper in small bowl; rub over both sides of salmon. Place salmon on top of vegetables in **CROCK-POT**® slow cooker. Pour Italian dressing over salmon; top with remaining bell peppers and onions. Add water. Cover; cook on HIGH 1½ hours.

3. Spread roll tops with chipotle mayonnaise and garnish with cilantro. Spoon 1 to 2 tablespoons cooking liquid onto roll bottoms. Place salmon fillet on each roll (remove skin first, if desired). Top with vegetable mixture.

best beef brisket sandwich ever

Makes 10 to 12 servings

- 1 beef brisket (about 3 pounds)*
- 2 cups apple cider, divided
- 1 head garlic, cloves separated, crushed and peeled
- ⅓ cup chopped fresh thyme *or* 2 tablespoons dried thyme
- 2 tablespoons whole black peppercorns
- 1 tablespoon mustard seeds
- 1 tablespoon Cajun seasoning
- 1 teaspoon ground allspice
- 1 teaspoon ground cumin
- 1 teaspoon celery seeds
- 2 to 4 whole cloves
- 1 can (12 ounces) dark beer
- 10 to 12 sourdough sandwich rolls, sliced in half

Unless you have a 5-, 6- or 7-quart **CROCK-POT® slow cooker, cut any roast larger than 2½ pounds in half so it cooks completely.*

1. Place brisket, ½ cup cider, garlic, thyme, peppercorns, mustard seeds, Cajun seasoning, allspice, cumin, celery seeds and cloves in large resealable food storage bag. Seal bag; turn to coat. Marinate in refrigerator overnight.

2. Place brisket and marinade in **CROCK-POT**® slow cooker. Add remaining 1½ cups cider and beer. Cover; cook on LOW 10 hours. Slice brisket and place on sandwich rolls. Drizzle cooking liquid over meat.

easy homemade barbecue sandwiches

Makes 8 servings

1 boneless pork butt roast (3 to 4 pounds)*
  Salt and black pepper
1 bottle (16 ounces) barbecue sauce
8 hamburger buns or sandwich rolls, toasted

*Unless you have a 5-, 6- or 7-quart **CROCK-POT**® slow cooker, cut any roast larger than 2½ pounds in half so it cooks completely.*

1. Pour water into bottom of **CROCK-POT**® slow cooker to depth of 1 inch. Season pork with salt and pepper; place in **CROCK-POT**® slow cooker. Cover; cook on LOW 8 to 10 hours.

2. Remove pork to large cutting board; shred with two forks. Discard cooking liquid. Turn **CROCK-POT**® slow cooker to HIGH. Return pork to **CROCK-POT**® slow cooker. Add barbecue sauce; stir to blend. Cover; cook on HIGH 30 minutes. Serve barbecue mixture on buns.

Note: Depending on the size of your roast, you may not need to use an entire bottle of barbecue sauce.

barbecued beef sandwiches

Makes 12 servings

  1 boneless beef chuck shoulder roast (about 3 pounds), trimmed*

  2 cups ketchup

  1 onion, chopped

  ¼ cup cider vinegar

  ¼ cup dark molasses

  2 tablespoons Worcestershire sauce

  2 cloves garlic, minced

  ½ teaspoon salt

  ½ teaspoon ground mustard

  ½ teaspoon black pepper

  ¼ teaspoon garlic powder

  ¼ teaspoon red pepper flakes

     Sesame seed buns, split

Unless you have a 5-, 6- or 7-quart **CROCK-POT® slow cooker, cut any roast larger than 2½ pounds in half so it cooks completely.*

1. Combine beef, ketchup, onion, vinegar, molasses, Worcestershire sauce, garlic, salt, mustard, black pepper, garlic powder and red pepper flakes in **CROCK-POT**® slow cooker. Cover; cook on LOW 8 to 10 hours or on HIGH 4 to 5 hours.

2. Turn off heat. Remove beef to large cutting board; shred with two forks. Let sauce stand 5 minutes. Skim off fat and discard.

3. Return shredded beef to **CROCK-POT**® slow cooker; stir to blend. Cover; cook on HIGH 10 to 15 minutes or until heated through. Spoon filling into buns and top with additional sauce, if desired.

shredded pork roast

Makes 8 to 10 servings

3½ to 4 pounds boneless pork shoulder, trimmed*
1 medium onion, finely chopped
⅔ cup ketchup
⅓ cup water
2 tablespoons chili powder
2 tablespoons packed brown sugar
1 tablespoon ground cumin
2 teaspoons garlic powder
1 teaspoon salt
1 teaspoon Worcestershire sauce
½ teaspoon black pepper
  Hoagie rolls
  Carrots and celery sticks (optional)

*Unless you have a 5-, 6- or 7-quart **CROCK-POT**® slow cooker, cut any roast larger than 2½ pounds in half so it cooks completely.*

1. Coat inside of **CROCK-POT**® slow cooker with nonstick cooking spray. Combine pork, onion, ketchup, water, chili powder, brown sugar, cumin, garlic powder, salt, Worcestershire sauce and pepper in **CROCK-POT**® slow cooker; turn pork to coat. Cover; cook on LOW 8 to 10 hours or on HIGH 4½ to 5 hours.

2. Remove pork to large bowl; shred with two forks, discarding fat. Pour ¾ cup cooking liquid into bowl; toss well. Serve pork in rolls. Serve with carrots and celery, if desired.

Note: If you like a saucier recipe, double the sauce recipe and reserve half for after cooking. When finished cooking, drain and discard cooking liquid. Shred meat; add new sauce. Cover; cook on HIGH 30 minutes or until heated through.

cheeseburger sloppy joes

Makes 6 to 8 servings

1½ pounds ground beef
  3 cloves garlic, minced
  1 small onion, finely chopped (about ½ cup)
  ½ cup ketchup
  ¼ cup water
  1 tablespoon packed brown sugar
  1 teaspoon Worcestershire sauce
  2 cups (8 ounces) shredded sharp Cheddar cheese
  6 to 8 hamburger rolls
    Carrot and celery sticks (optional)

1. Coat inside of **CROCK-POT**® slow cooker with nonstick cooking spray. Brown beef in large skillet over medium-high heat 6 to 8 minutes, stirring to break up meat. Drain fat. Stir in garlic and onion; cook and stir 3 to 4 minutes.

2. Add beef mixture, ketchup, water, brown sugar and Worcestershire sauce to **CROCK-POT**® slow cooker; stir to blend. Cover; cook on LOW 4 to 5 hours or on HIGH 2 to 2½ hours. Stir in cheese until melted. Serve on rolls with carrot and celery sticks, if desired.

hot beef sandwiches

Makes 6 to 8 servings

1 boneless beef chuck roast (3 to 4 pounds), trimmed*
1 can (about 14 ounces) crushed tomatoes with Italian seasoning
1 jar (6 ounces) sliced dill pickles, undrained
1 onion, diced
4 cloves garlic, minced
1 teaspoon mustard seeds
  Hamburger buns
  Toppings: lettuce, tomato slices and red onion slices

*Unless you have a 5-, 6- or 7-quart **CROCK-POT®** slow cooker, cut any roast larger than 2½ pounds in half so it cooks completely.*

1. Combine beef, tomatoes, pickles, onion, garlic and mustard seeds in **CROCK-POT®** slow cooker; stir to blend. Cover; cook on LOW 8 to 10 hours.

2. Remove beef to large cutting board; shred with two forks. Return shreddred beef to **CROCK-POT®** slow cooker; stir to blend. Top buns with lettuce, tomato, beef and pickle mixture, onion slices and bun tops.

sloppy joe sliders

Makes 24 mini sandwiches

1 pound ground beef
1 can (about 14 ounces) stewed tomatoes with Mexican seasoning
½ cup frozen mixed vegetables
½ cup chopped green bell pepper
3 tablespoons ketchup
2 teaspoons Worcestershire sauce
1 teaspoon *each* ground cumin and cider vinegar
24 mini whole wheat rolls, split and warmed

1. Brown beef in large skillet over medium-high heat 6 to 8 minutes, stirring to break up meat. Remove to **CROCK-POT®** slow cooker using slotted spoon.

2. Add tomatoes, mixed vegetables, bell pepper, ketchup, Worcestershire sauce, cumin and vinegar. Cover; cook on LOW 2 to 3 hours. Serve on rolls.

hot beef sandwiches

cuban pork sandwiches

Makes 8 servings

    Nonstick cooking spray
1 pork loin roast (about 2 pounds)
½ cup orange juice
2 tablespoons lime juice
1 tablespoon minced garlic
1½ teaspoons salt
½ teaspoon red pepper flakes
8 crusty bread rolls, split in half (6 inches *each*)
2 tablespoons yellow mustard
8 slices Swiss cheese
8 thin ham slices
4 small dill pickles, thinly sliced lengthwise

1. Coat inside of **CROCK-POT®** slow cooker with nonstick cooking spray. Add pork loin.

2. Combine orange juice, lime juice, garlic, salt and red pepper flakes in small bowl; stir to blend. Pour over pork. Cover; cook on LOW 7 to 8 hours or on HIGH 3½ to 4 hours. Remove pork to large cutting board. Cover loosely with foil; let stand 10 to 15 minutes before slicing.

3. To serve, spread mustard on both sides of rolls. Divide pork slices among roll bottoms. Top with Swiss cheese slice, ham slice and pickle slices; cover with tops of rolls.

4. Coat large skillet with cooking spray; heat over medium heat. Working in batches, arrange sandwiches in skillet. Cover with foil; top with dinner plate to press down sandwiches. (If necessary, weigh down with 2 to 3 cans to compress sandwiches lightly.) Cook 8 minutes or until cheese is melted.*

*Or use table top grill to compress and heat sandwiches.

super meatball sliders

Makes 24 sliders

1 can (15 ounces) whole berry cranberry sauce
1 can (about 15 ounces) tomato sauce
⅛ teaspoon red pepper flakes (optional)
2 pounds ground beef or turkey
¾ cup dry seasoned bread crumbs
1 egg, lightly beaten
1 package (1 ounce) dry onion soup mix
   Nonstick cooking spray
   Baby arugula leaves (optional)
24 small potato rolls or dinner rolls
6 slices (1 ounce *each*) provolone cheese, cut into quarters

1. Combine cranberry sauce, tomato sauce and red pepper flakes, if desired, in **CROCK-POT**® slow cooker. Cover; cook on LOW 3 to 4 hours.

2. Halfway through cooking time, prepare meatballs. Combine beef, bread crumbs, egg and dry soup mix in large bowl; mix well. Shape mixture into 24 (1¾-inch) meatballs. Spray medium skillet with cooking spray; heat over medium heat. Add meatballs; cook 8 to 10 minutes or until browned on all sides. Remove meatballs to **CROCK-POT**® slow cooker.

3. Cover; cook on LOW 1 to 2 hours or until meatballs are no longer pink in centers. Place arugula leaves on bottom of rolls, if desired; top with meatballs and cheese. Spoon sauce over meatballs; cover with roll tops.

big al's hot and sweet sausage sandwiches

Makes 8 to 10 servings

4 to 5 pounds hot Italian sausage links
1 jar (26 ounces) pasta sauce
1 large Vidalia onion (or other sweet onion), sliced
1 green bell pepper, sliced
1 red bell pepper, sliced
¼ cup packed dark brown sugar
 Provolone cheese, sliced
 Italian rolls, cut in half

Combine sausages, pasta sauce, onion, bell peppers and brown sugar in **CROCK-POT**® slow cooker. Cover; cook on LOW 8 to 10 hours or on HIGH 4 to 6 hours. Place cheese and sausage on rolls. Top with vegetable mixture.

bbq pulled chicken sandwiches

Makes 4 servings

1¼ to 1½ pounds boneless, skinless chicken thighs
1 package (14 ounces) frozen bell pepper and onion strips cut for stir-fry
¾ cup barbecue sauce, divided
¼ to ½ teaspoon hot pepper sauce
4 Kaiser rolls, split and toasted

1. Combine chicken, bell pepper and onion strips and ¼ cup barbecue sauce in **CROCK-POT**® slow cooker; stir to blend. Cover; cook on LOW 5 to 6 hours or on HIGH 2 to 3 hours.

2. Remove chicken to medium bowl; shred with two forks. Drain pepper mixture; add to bowl with chicken. Add remaining ½ cup barbecue sauce and hot pepper sauce; stir to blend. Serve in rolls.

big al's hot and sweet
sausage sandwiches

barbecue beef sliders

Makes 6 servings

  1 tablespoon packed light brown sugar
  1 teaspoon ground cumin
  1 teaspoon chili powder
  1 teaspoon paprika
  ½ teaspoon salt
  ¼ teaspoon ground red pepper
  3 pounds boneless beef short ribs
  ½ cup plus 2 tablespoons barbecue sauce, divided
  ¼ cup water
12 slider rolls
  ¾ cup prepared coleslaw
12 bread and butter pickle chips
    Potato chips (optional)

1. Coat inside of **CROCK-POT®** slow cooker with nonstick cooking spray. Combine brown sugar, cumin, chili powder, paprika, salt and ground red pepper in small bowl; stir to blend. Rub over ribs. Remove to **CROCK-POT®** slow cooker. Pour in ½ cup barbecue sauce and ¼ cup water.

2. Cover; cook on LOW 7 to 8 hours or on HIGH 4 to 4½ hours. Remove ribs to large bowl; shred with two forks, discarding any fat. Stir in remaining 2 tablespoons barbecue sauce and 2 tablespoons liquid from **CROCK-POT®** slow cooker.

3. Arrange bottom half of rolls on large platter. Top each with beef mixture, coleslaw, pickle chip and roll top. Serve with potato chips, if desired.

Tip: To remove remaining sticky barbecue sauce residue, soak the **CROCK-POT®** stoneware in hot sudsy water and then scrub it with a plastic or nylon scrubber. Don't use steel wool.

italian meatball hoagies

Makes 4 servings

½ pound lean ground beef
½ pound Italian sausage, casings removed
¼ cup Italian seasoned dry bread crumbs
¼ cup grated Parmesan cheese
1 egg
1 tablespoon olive oil
1 cup pasta sauce
2 tablespoons tomato paste
¼ teaspoon red pepper flakes (optional)
4 (6-inch) hoagie rolls, split and lightly toasted
1 cup (4 ounces) shredded mozzarella cheese

1. Coat inside of **CROCK-POT**® slow cooker with nonstick cooking spray. Combine ground beef, sausage, bread crumbs, Parmesan cheese and egg in large bowl; mix well. Shape to form 16 (1½-inch) meatballs.

2. Heat oil in large skillet over medium heat. Add meatballs; cook 6 to 8 minutes or until browned on all sides, turning occasionally. Remove meatballs to **CROCK-POT**® slow cooker using slotted spoon.

3. Combine pasta sauce, tomato paste and red pepper flakes, if desired, in medium bowl; stir to blend. Spoon over meatballs; gently toss with sauce.

4. Cover; cook on LOW 5 to 7 hours or on HIGH 2½ to 3 hours. Place meatballs in rolls. Spoon sauce over meatballs; top with mozzarella cheese.

hot beef sandwiches au jus

Makes 8 to 10 servings

    4 pounds boneless beef bottom round roast, trimmed*
    2 cans (about 10 ounces *each*) condensed beef broth, undiluted
    1 can (12 ounces) beer
    2 envelopes (1 ounce *each*) dried onion-flavor soup mix
    1 tablespoon minced garlic
    2 teaspoons sugar
    1 teaspoon dried oregano
       Crusty French rolls, sliced in half

Unless you have a 5-, 6- or 7-quart **CROCK-POT® slow cooker, cut any roast larger than 2½ pounds in half so it cooks completely.*

1. Combine beef, broth, beer, dry soup mix, garlic, sugar and oregano in **CROCK-POT**® slow cooker. Cover; cook on HIGH 6 to 8 hours.

2. Remove beef to large cutting board; shred with two forks. Return beef to cooking liquid; stir to blend. Serve on rolls with cooking liquid for dipping.

hot beef sandwiches au jus

meatless sloppy joes

Makes 4 servings

- 2 cups thinly sliced onions
- 2 cups chopped green bell peppers
- 1 can (about 15 ounces) kidney beans, drained and mashed
- 1 can (8 ounces) tomato sauce
- 2 tablespoons ketchup
- 1 tablespoon yellow mustard
- 2 cloves garlic, finely chopped
- 1 teaspoon chili powder
- 1 tablespoon cider vinegar (optional)
- 4 sandwich rolls
  Carrot sticks (optional)

Combine onions, bell peppers, beans, tomato sauce, ketchup, mustard, garlic and chili powder in **CROCK-POT**® slow cooker; stir to blend. Cover; cook on LOW 5 to 5½ hours. Add vinegar, if desired. Serve on rolls with carrots, if desired.

green chile pulled pork sandwiches

Makes 8 servings

3½ to 4 pounds boneless pork shoulder roast, trimmed*
1 teaspoon salt
½ teaspoon black pepper
1 can (about 14 ounces) diced tomatoes with mild green chiles
1 cup chopped onion
½ cup water
2 tablespoons lime juice
1 teaspoon ground cumin
1 teaspoon minced garlic
2 canned chipotle peppers in adobo sauce, minced
8 hard rolls or hoagie buns
½ cup sour cream
2 avocados, sliced
3 tablespoons chopped fresh cilantro (optional)

*Unless you have a 5-, 6- or 7-quart **CROCK-POT**® slow cooker, cut any roast larger than 2½ pounds in half so it cooks completely.

1. Season pork with salt and black pepper. Place pork in **CROCK-POT**® slow cooker.

2. Combine tomatoes, onion, water, lime juice, cumin, garlic and chipotle peppers in medium bowl. Pour over pork in **CROCK-POT**® slow cooker. Cover; cook on LOW 7 to 8 hours.

3. Remove pork to large cutting board; shred with two forks, discarding any fat. Return to cooking liquid; stir to combine. Serve on rolls. Top with sour cream, avocado and cilantro, if desired.

hoisin barbecue chicken sliders

Makes 16 sliders

⅔ cup hoisin sauce

⅓ cup barbecue sauce

3 tablespoons quick-cooking tapioca

1 tablespoon sugar

1 tablespoon soy sauce

¼ teaspoon red pepper flakes

12 boneless, skinless chicken thighs (3 to 3½ pounds total)

16 dinner rolls or Hawaiian sweet rolls, split

½ medium red onion, finely chopped (optional)

Sliced pickles (optional)

1. Combine hoisin sauce, barbecue sauce, tapioca, sugar, soy sauce and red pepper flakes in **CROCK-POT**® slow cooker; stir to blend. Add chicken. Cover; cook on LOW 8 to 9 hours.

2. Remove chicken to large cutting board; shred with two forks. Return shredded chicken to **CROCK-POT**® slow cooker; stir to blend. Spoon chicken and sauce onto each roll. Top with chopped onion and pickles, if desired.

sloppy sloppy joes

Makes 20 to 25 servings

- 4 pounds ground beef
- 1 cup chopped onion
- 1 cup chopped green bell pepper
- 1 can (about 28 ounces) tomato sauce
- 2 cans (10¾ ounces *each*) condensed tomato soup, undiluted
- 1 cup packed brown sugar
- ¼ cup ketchup
- 3 tablespoons Worcestershire sauce
- 1 tablespoon ground mustard
- 1 tablespoon prepared mustard
- 1½ teaspoons chili powder
- 1 teaspoon garlic powder
- Toasted hamburger buns
- Potato chips (optional)

1. Brown beef in large skillet over medium-high heat 6 to 8 minutes, stirring to break up meat. Drain fat. Add onion and bell pepper; cook and stir 5 to 10 minutes or until onion is translucent. Remove mixture to **CROCK-POT®** slow cooker.

2. Add tomato sauce, tomato soup, brown sugar, ketchup, Worcestershire sauce, ground mustard, prepared mustard, chili powder and garlic powder; stir to blend. Cover; cook on LOW 4 to 6 hours. Serve on buns with chips, if desired.

barbecued pulled pork sandwiches

Makes 8 servings

- 1 boneless pork shoulder roast (2½ pounds), trimmed
- 1 bottle (14 ounces) barbecue sauce
- 1 tablespoon lemon juice
- 1 teaspoon packed brown sugar
- 1 medium onion, chopped
  Sandwich rolls or hamburger buns

1. Place pork in **CROCK-POT**® slow cooker. Cover; cook on LOW 10 to 12 hours or on HIGH 5 to 6 hours.

2. Remove pork to large cutting board; shred with two forks. Discard cooking liquid. Return pork to **CROCK-POT**® slow cooker; add barbecue sauce, lemon juice, brown sugar and onion. Cover; cook on LOW 2 hours or on HIGH 1 hour. Serve pork on rolls.

Serving Suggestion: Serve with crunchy coleslaw on the side.

Tip: For a 5-, 6- or 7-quart **CROCK-POT**® slow cooker, double all ingredients, except for the barbecue sauce. Increase the barbecue sauce to 1½ bottles (about 21 ounces total).